LEGENDS OF NORSE MYTHOLOGY

WIDE EYED EDITIONS

INTRODUCTION

In the Norse homelands, the winters are cold and harsh, the seas are icy and the short summers burst with life. It is easy to imagine frost giants in the mountains and sea monsters beneath the waves, or to look at a rainbow and picture a bridge to another world. The Norse myths were passed down by the people who lived in these lands during Viking times. They used these stories to explain how the world was made, and how it would end: the gods, giants, and mythical beings collected in this book helped people make sense of their lives and inspired them to great adventures.

Some of the gods and monsters you'll meet in these pages might already be familiar: burly Thor with his powerful hammer, or mischievous, shape-shifting Loki. You may have come across elves and dwarfs in books and films inspired by the same stories. But there is a lot that might surprise you as well—from the goddess who cried tears of gold and rode a chariot pulled by cats, to the serpent that encircled the whole world. The Norse myths are some of the most remarkable stories ever told, with a colorful cast of characters.

Welcome to the extraordinary world of the Norse imagination!

Most of what we know about Norse mythology comes from poetry and sagas. These stories were passed down from generation to generation, and the language of these original tales is Old Norse. In this book, the more familiar English names are used.

There are many different ways of understanding the myths. Sometimes these stories help us to understand ourselves, what we're scared of, and why we do the things we do. But above all, the Norse myths are timeless tales just waiting to be told . . .

CONTENTS

THE STORY OF THE NINE WORLDS — 4

THE GODS — 6

Odin	8	Heimdall	24
Frigg	10	Tyr	26
Thor	12	Sif	28
Loki	14	Bragi & Idun	30
Baldur	16	Njörd & Skadi	32
Mimir	18	Gullveig	34
Freyr	20	The Children of the Gods	36
Freyja	22		

THE STORY OF THOR'S HAMMER — 38

THE STORY OF POETRY — 40

GIANTS, MONSTERS, AND MYTHICAL BEINGS — 42

Aegir & Ran	44	The Valkyries	60
Hrungnir	46	Elves	62
Thrym	48	Huginn & Muninn	64
Utgarda-Loki	50	The Norns	66
Gjalp & Greip	52	Hel	68
Fenja & Menja	54	Jörmungand	70
Dwarfs	56	Fenrir	72
Sleipnir	58	Surt	74

THE STORY OF RAGNARÖK — 76

GLOSSARY — 78

THE STORY OF THE NINE WORLDS

There were nine worlds in the Norse cosmos. The oldest were Niflheim, the realm of frost, and Muspellsheim, the realm of fire.

Between them stretched a gaping void called Ginnungagap, where rivers of ice flowing from Niflheim met the heat of Muspellsheim, and warm mists swirled. Out of these mists stepped the giant Ymir. Ymir was the first being in the entire cosmos, but not for long.

A cow called Audhumla emerged from the mists, and Ymir fed on her milk. Next, Ymir—who was neither man nor woman—lay down to sleep, and from the sweat that formed in those huge armpits, the first giants were born. Soon there were many giants walking through the mists.

The cow Audhumla had been busy licking at the salty ice that covered Ginnungagap, and from the melting frost emerged a god called Buri. Buri's grandsons were the brothers Odin, Vili, and Ve, and they wondered how to build a better world than this harsh, misty land. They decided to kill Ymir and use the giant's enormous body as their building material.

From Ymir's blood, the gods created oceans and lakes. Odin fixed Ymir's skull above the world to make the sky, and used the giant's brains to create the billowing clouds. Ymir's bones became the mountains, the stubble on Ymir's face became the tall pine trees, and the giant's teeth were ground into powder and scattered across the world as grit and sand. Finally, the gods took Ymir's eyelashes and made a barrier to protect the world they had just made. They called this place Midgard, the middle earth—the same world that humans live in today.

The gods had their own realm above ours called Asgard and it was filled with golden halls and spendid temples. The only way to reach it was via the rainbow bridge, which connected the worlds of humans and gods. Some gods also came from a land called Vanaheim, which was so far away that no one remembers how to get there.

The giants lived in Jötunheim, a land of towering mountains and desolate lava fields far away across raging rivers that never froze. Other beings had their own realms, too. The elves lived beneath the bright skies of Alfheim, and the dwarfs in the caverns and caves of Svartalfheim. Finally, the last of the nine worlds was also the most feared—this was Hel, the home of the dead.

Through all nine worlds grew a tree with roots that sank far beneath the ground and with branches that reached up high into the heavens. This was Yggdrasil, the mighty, measureless World-Tree.

THE GODS

From shape-shifting Loki to the mysterious golden Gullveig, the Norse gods took many different forms.

Odin, the All-Father, was the head of the Aesir family of gods, and his wife was the far-seeing Frigg. Their most famous son was Thor, who battled giants with his hammer and kept the world safe. Another family of gods, the Vanir, were powerful in life-giving magic, especially Njörd's two children Freyr and Freyja, who helped with love and new life. The two families once fought each other, but made peace when they realized that neither side could win! Like any big family, the gods had their squabbles and their rivalries, but they worked together when threatened by giants, and they protected humans from the world-destroying monsters.

The Norse gods may have had awesome powers, but they weren't immortal or untouchable: Odin had one eye and traveled the world disguised as an old man, Tyr had one hand and Mimir had no body. They each had amazing abilities, but also their own flaws. Thor was superstrong, but had no control over his temper, and Freyja was dazzlingly beautiful, but treated her lovers like a cat taunting mice. Loki was the trickiest of all: their father was a giant, and no one was ever sure what side they were on.

Some of the gods had specific tasks: Heimdall guarded the rainbow bridge and Bragi was the poet; Idun kept the rest of the gods young, and Njörd controlled the seas. Sif represented the family and Tyr was the god of war.

There was one thing more powerful than the gods and that was the fate that controls all lives. Even the gods could not escape their destiny, no matter how hard they tried.

"All-Father, ancient-one, wanderer, friend of the slain: Odin was known by countless different names."

ODIN

THE ALL-FATHER, LEADER OF THE NORSE GODS AND LORD OF THE GALLOWS

WHERE: *Valhalla, or walking the world disguised as a weary old man*

Odin was known as the father of the gods. With his brothers Villi and Ve, he created the entire world from the body of the giant Ymir and breathed life into the first humans. The All-Father's memory stretched back almost as far as time itself, and wise Odin valued knowledge more than any treasure. He sacrificed one of his eyes so that he'd be able to see things hidden in the mists of time, and he once hung from the World-Tree for nine nights just to learn the secrets of the runes. From his seeing-seat Hlidskjalf, Odin could look out across the nine worlds and very little escaped his one bright eye.

Odin knew many things that are hidden from humans. He knew spells that could charm the sharpness out of weapons and spells to raise the dead and make them speak. What's more, he could fix the outcome of a battle before it even began. More than any other god, Odin enjoyed traveling through the human world in disguise and meddling in people's lives. If an old man with a long beard and a wide-brimmed hat came to your home, it was best to be on guard!

As the leader of the gods, Odin was always respected, but he was not trusted—even by the people who worshiped him. He tricked many proud rulers into contests that they could never win, and he was unfaithful to all of his lovers. Odin made the career of many a hero or king and gave them all that they desired, but he could just as easily take everything away. The father of the gods did not like playing by the rules.

◊ Odin's hall was Valhalla, the hall of the slain, which was roofed with golden shields that sparkled in the sun. It was to Valhalla that the warrior women known as the Valkyries brought the bravest of those who died in battle to feast and fight in preparation for war with the giants.

◊ Odin had two ravens called Huginn and Muninn that he sent out across the worlds to bring him news, and two wolves that he fed beneath his table. He owned a magic ring named Draupnir, and his weapon was the spear Gungnir, which he threw to start the first war in the world.

FRIGG

QUEEN AMONG THE GODDESSES; SHE GAVE HER NAME TO FRIDAY

WHERE: *The hall Fensalir, surrounded by marsh and wetlands*

Frigg was the most important of all the goddesses. When the gods held a feast, she sat beside her husband Odin in the place of honor. She was served by two loyal handmaidens called Fulla and Gna. Frigg had the gift of foresight and knew the fates of many gods.

Neither Odin nor Frigg were particularly faithful to each other and they fought often: there were even rumors that Odin was banished from Asgard for a while because of the way he treated his lovers, and that Frigg became wife to both Odin's brothers when he was away. When Frigg and Odin took different sides in a contest, it was never clear who would win. After one argument, Frigg set a trap for Odin that led to him being mistaken for a sorcerer and captured by his enemies! However, despite their many quarrels, Frigg would still shed tears for her husband when he finally met his end and was swallowed by the giant wolf Fenrir.

Frigg was worshipped by all people, but particularly by mothers. She had many famous children, but her favorite was Baldur, the shining god. When Baldur was a baby, Frigg was so scared of losing him that she made every living thing swear an oath not to harm him. The only thing she forgot to ask was the lowly mistletoe, which ended up being the plant that killed him, when his brother Höd was tricked into throwing a mistletoe dart at Baldur's chest. Frigg was overcome with grief when Baldur died, and she used her mighty power to command every living thing to weep for him in the hope this would release him from Hel.

◊ People thought Frigg was the equivalent of the powerful Roman goddess Venus. Because of this, her name was given to Venus's day: we know this day as Frigg's Day, or Friday.

◊ Frigg was also a healer and was able to charm Baldur's horse back to life when it took a fall. To do this she worked with her husband and not against him—for a change!

◊ It was only the trickster god Loki, disguised as an old woman, who resisted Frigg's power and refused to shed a tear for Baldur, leaving him stuck in Hel.

"When the names of all the goddesses were listed, Frigg's was always the first."

THOR

THE HAMMER-WIELDING SON OF ODIN AND PROTECTOR OF THE GODS

WHERE: *In his lightning-struck hall, or pursuing giants in Jötunheim*

No god was mightier than Thor, wielder of the hammer Mjölnir. Odin's red-bearded son was not afraid to take on opponents many times his size and he was always looking for a fight. Thor was in charge of protecting the realm of the gods and the human world from both giants and terrifying monsters. He was worshipped by everyone, but particularly warriors who admired his awesome strength. Thor also protected sailors and fishermen, and he was famous for hooking the giant Midgard-Serpent that lay at the bottom of the ocean on his fishing line.

If Thor had a weakness, it was his temper, which sometimes got the better of him. He was so angry when his hammer was stolen by the giant Thrym that he killed the giant's aunts and in-laws as well as the thief himself. His temper even led to him being tricked into wrestling with old age itself in the home of the giant Utgarda-Loki—this was a fight that even mighty Thor couldn't win. Odin sometimes took pleasure in teasing his hot-headed son, but only when he was well out of Thor's reach! All the gods knew that Thor was a fierce opponent and he was usually treated with respect.

Sometimes Loki accompanied Thor on his adventures in giant land, and sometimes he was joined by his two human servants Thjalfi and Röskva. Wherever their journeys took them, it usually resulted in the battling of giants. Thor's mother was the earth giantess Jörd, but this didn't change his feelings toward the rest of his giant relatives.

◊ Thor's weapon was the famous hammer Mjölnir, which never missed its target. He also owned a pair of iron gloves that helped him to wield the hammer, and a belt of power that increased his awesome strength. Some Vikings wore hammer pendants around their necks to call on Thor's protection.

◊ A terrible end waits for Thor: he is destined to fight the Midgard-Serpent at Ragnarök (see page 76). His fate is to kill the monster, but he will only take nine steps before dying from its poison.

"Without Thor and his awesome strength, the worlds of gods and humans would soon have been overrun by giants and monsters."

LOKI

THE TRICKSTER GOD: MISCHIEF MAKER AND PARENT OF MONSTROUS CHILDREN

WHERE: *Wherever there was trouble*

Loki was an outsider and a shape-shifter who was as comfortable in the body of an old woman as they were in the body of a young man. Loki's father was a giant and their mother was a goddess called Laufey, which broke all the gods' rules about marriage: though giantesses could marry into the Aesir family, unions with male giants were off-limits. Loki lived with the gods in Asgard, but no one was ever sure of their loyalties. Sometimes they helped the gods and sometimes they worked with the giants. Other times, Loki just made trouble for fun. Loki's quick thinking often helped other gods out of tricky situations . . . but usually they were the one to have caused the problem in the first place!

Loki owned a pair of shoes that allowed them to run through the air. The trickster god could change their shape, taking the form of a seal, a salmon, a horse, and even a tiny biting fly. They also had the ability to change their human form as easily as changing clothes. Once, they even gave birth to a beautiful eight-legged horse called Sleipnir! Loki's loyal wife was Sigyn, but Loki also had a lover who was a troll woman living in the Iron Woods. From this union came three monstrous children: the enormous serpent Jörmungand, the wolf Fenrir, and a fierce daughter named Hel.

The gods tolerated Loki for a long time, but eventually Loki committed a crime so serious that they couldn't ignore the mischief any longer. Loki was the mastermind behind Baldur's death, and for this Loki was chained beneath the earth with a snake tied over their head to drip poison in their eyes. Lying in their chains, Loki had a long time to plan revenge on the gods. When Ragnarök comes, Loki will be ready to lead the forces of chaos across the ocean to Asgard.

◊ Loki's wife Sigyn showed her love by catching the poison in a bowl before it could drip into Loki's eyes. But now and then she had to leave to empty the bowl, and when she did, the god's pain caused earthquakes across the world.

◊ Loki loved gossip and knew the secrets of many of the gods. At one feast, they managed to insult every single god and goddess by sharing their most embarrassing stories. But all of them were true!

◊ Loki will fight on the side of the giants at the great battle Ragnarök, piloting a ship made from all the nail clippings ever thrown away. The Vikings believed that nail clippings had to be burned: otherwise Loki's ship would be built too quickly!

"If one thing comforted Loki while they were imprisoned, it was the thought that their children would destroy the world the gods had made."

"The loss of Baldur the beautiful was the greatest tragedy to befall the gods; at least until Ragnarök comes and sweeps the old world away."

BALDUR

THE BRIGHT AND SHINING GOD, WHOSE DEATH WAS MOURNED BY THE WHOLE WORLD

WHERE: *In his hall Breidablik, and later holding court in Hel*

Baldur was Odin's second son. He represented all the best qualities of the Aesir family through his gentleness and fairness. His skin was so bright that it shone like the sky, and his hair and eyebrows were so pale that they looked whiter than the whitest of flowers. No one had a bad word to say about Baldur, and everywhere he went, people spoke of the beauty of his voice, his wisdom, and his kindness . . . even though they often forgot to follow his advice.

When Baldur was born, his mother Frigg made everything around her, including forest fires, floods, fierce animals, and poisonous serpents, swear not to harm him. These oaths were so sacred that even lifeless objects obeyed the rules, and the gods amused themselves by throwing things at Baldur to see them bounce harmlessly away. But Frigg forgot to ask one small and harmless plant to swear the oath: the mistletoe. It was an arrow made by Loki from this very plant that killed the shining god.

Baldur's funeral was the greatest ever held across the nine worlds. He was placed in his huge longship Ringhorn with so much treasure that a giantess's strength was needed to push the ship into the water. From there it was set alight and burned brightly against the gray sky.

It's a sign of Baldur's goodness that all living things wept when he died. Only one, an old woman who was probably Loki in disguise, refused to weep. For this reason, Baldur was not allowed to leave the land of the dead. He will wait many years as the guest of Hel until the great battle of Ragnarök before he can return to Asgard. When the world is reborn, Baldur will bathe the home of the gods with his brightness once again.

◊ Before he died, Baldur began to have bad dreams. Odin raised a giantess from the dead to question her about Baldur's nightmares. Even though he learned that Baldur was destined to be killed by his own brother, the father of the gods was powerless to change his son's fate.

◊ When Baldur died, even lifeless stone and iron wept. It was once believed that this is why, when we leave something metal outside overnight, in the morning we find it glistening with moisture and running with tears for Baldur.

◊ Baldur's loyal wife Nanna was so sad at his funeral that she died from a broken heart, and the gods laid her on the same funeral pyre as her husband. Baldur and Nanna walked hand in hand into Hel's realm.

MIMIR

A WISE GOD GIVEN AS A HOSTAGE TO THE VANIR; HE ADVISED ODIN ON ALL THINGS

WHERE: *Staring up from the water of the sacred well*

Mimir the wise was a close friend to Odin. During the golden age of the gods, Mimir drank from the well of wisdom while the gods around him built bright temples and feasted, and he became the wisest of the Aesir. When the mysterious golden Gullveig arrived in Asgard, Mimir predicted that trouble would come from her family, the Vanir. Mimir was there when Odin threw his spear and started a war against these rival gods, and it was he who realized that the Vanir family could not be killed and that neither side could win.

When the Aesir and the Vanir gods called a truce in their fighting, they exchanged oaths and hostages and wise Mimir was chosen to go as a hostage to the realm of Vanaheim with the noble but shy god Hœnir. The two got on well at first: when Mimir was there to give him advice, Hœnir acted like the noble god he was. However, whenever Mimir was away, Hœnir refused to speak. The Vanir gods thought they'd been cheated because one of their hostages couldn't do a thing without the other, and so they chopped off Mimir's head and sent it back to Odin to let him know how angry they were that they'd been short-changed.

Odin knew herbs and spells that would preserve Mimir's head and allow his old friend to speak. Odin placed the head in the sacred well where Mimir used to drink, and he often came to the well to talk with his wise friend and benefit from his advice. Mimir was said to be particularly good with runes, but no one really knew all the secrets contained within that time-wrinkled old head.

◊ Before he was taken hostage, Mimir drank each morning at a well beneath the roots of the World-Tree, using a gold drinking vessel called the Gjallarhorn. Later known as Mimir's well, this became one of Odin's favorite places to go and think.

◊ No one quite knows what happened to Hœnir, but it is said he will be one of the few gods to survive Ragnarök and enjoy the new world—which is probably better than losing your head!

"There was almost nothing that wise Mimir didn't already know, but even he couldn't change the fate of the gods."

FREYR

GOD OF THE FIELDS AND FERTILITY, WHO RODE A SHINING GOLD BOAR

WHERE: *In Alfheim, the bright home of the elves*

Freyr, like his father the sea god Njörd, his sister Freyja, and the rest of the Vanir family, was a god of fertility. He helped fields to grow and crops to ripen. Without Freyr the world would have been a barren place and he was held in high regard by everyone, but particularly worshipped by farmers and people who lived from the land.

One fateful day, Freyr decided to sit in Odin's seeing-seat Hlidskjalf—a place he absolutely was not supposed to go. Looking out across the worlds, he saw a beautiful giantess with shining arms and fell hopelessly in love. He was so lovesick that he wouldn't eat or sleep. His father Njörd grew more and more worried for his son, but Freyr wouldn't tell anyone the reason why he looked so unwell. Eventually Freyr's loyal servant Skirnir traveled down from the sky to giant land, like a sunbeam breaking from a cloud. He found the beautiful giantess, whose name was Gerd, and after a lot of threats he bullied her into meeting his master and becoming his wife, and the color finally returned to Freyr's cheeks. In matters of love, the gods always wanted to get their own way.

Freyr owned a magic sword that could fight by itself, but he lost it when he gave it to Skirnir to help protect him on his journey to find Gerd. For this reason, Freyr is destined to meet the fire giant Surt in the final battle at Ragnarök without a sword. Though Surt will slay the god of the fields, Freyr will fight bravely until the end.

◊ Freyr's most precious objects were the golden boar Gullinbursti, which pulled his chariot through the air and lit up the night sky, and the fabulous longship Skidbladnir, which could be folded up so small that the god could carry it in his pocket.

◊ When Freyr grew his first tooth as a baby, he was given the gift of the bright realm of Alfheim as a present. This was also the home of the elves and was said to be far up in the heavens where the air is thin and the light is brightest.

◊ Farmers sometimes placed a wooden statue of Freyr in a chariot and processed it from home to home in hope that their crops would grow well.

"Warming sunshine, rich earth, gentle rain: these were signs that Freyr had blessed the land."

"Freyja's name was on the lips of every lover, and in the mind of everyone hoping for love."

Freyja once agreed to help a faithful follower of hers to discover his ancestry: to do this she turned him into a boar with golden bristles and rode him to the home of a giantess who knew all about his family. Freyja helped him because he built a stone altar in her honor and only made sacrifices to her.

FREYJA

THE MOST DESIRING AND DESIRED OF THE GODS, CALLED ON IN MATTERS OF LOVE

WHERE: *In her hall, Sessrumnir, and wherever her heart took her*

Freyja, the sister of Freyr, was the goddess of fertility and love. She was known throughout the nine worlds for both her beauty and her love of precious things. Freyja came to Asgard from Vanaheim, and she taught the gods about the most forbidden of magic arts and the true power of desire. She had many lovers and was always on the lookout for more.

Freyja could be recognized by her elaborate necklace and her fabulous falcon-feather cloak, as well as by her cart pulled by graceful cats. She ruled over the field known as Folkvang, where half of all the warriors who died in battle were brought by the Valkyries to spend their afterlife feasting and preparing for Ragnarök. Freyja had a well-furnished hall called Sessrumnir there, where she lived a life of pleasure. Freyja was known to have relationships with humans: it helped when she received the gift of a love poem, which she found very hard to resist. But none of her lovers expected to keep her attention for long: she snorted with laughter if anyone suggested that she give up her freedom to love whoever she wanted!

Of all the goddesses, it was beautiful Freyja who the giants most wanted to kidnap and carry away to their stone homes, but Freyja exploded with rage at the merest mention of her traveling to Jötunheim or having anything to do with a giant, and no one in the nine worlds could make Freyja do something she didn't want to do.

◊ Freyja was once surprised by a god bursting into her bedroom, and was so shocked at the intrusion that she let out a fart! But Freyja did not like to be reminded of this embarrassing story, and only Loki was mean enough to mention it in public.

◊ Freyja's husband, Od, left one day to go traveling and never returned. As brave as she was, Freyja still cried when she was alone, and the tears were said to turn into red gold. Her daughters with Od were called Hnoss and Gersimi, and both their names mean "treasure."

◊ Freyja owned the Brisingamen, which was the most elaborate necklace ever made. Loki the trickster god stole it from her and her anger at their boldness shook the heavens.

"Whether it was the sound of growing grass, or the beating of a moth's wings in the world below: nothing escaped the watchman's attention."

HEIMDALL

THE WATCHMAN OF THE GODS, CHARGED WITH GUARDING THE RAINBOW BRIDGE

WHERE: *Sitting beneath the World-Tree, watching over the worlds below*

Heimdall was the gatekeeper of Asgard, and the guardian of Bifröst, the rainbow bridge that connected the world of humans to the world of the gods. Heimdall was said to have been born to nine mothers and was blessed with incredible eyesight and hearing. He could see as clearly in the pitch-black night as he could in the middle of the day and could even hear the wool growing on a sheep's back. Heimdall was sometimes called the whitest of the gods, perhaps because he sat on guard with his back against the World-Tree and became covered in sticky white clay.

It was hard to miss Heimdall because his mouth was filled with golden teeth. He also carried the magnificent golden Gjallarhorn, which was once used by the god Mimir to drink from the well of knowledge. Heimdall would blow on the Gjallarhorn to warn the gods that giants were approaching the rainbow bridge. As a watchman, he needed as little sleep as a bird, which was a good thing, since he had to guard the bridge at all times.

Using a different name, Heimdall once visited the human world, and spent the night at three different houses: the hut of a peasant couple, the homestead of two farmers, and the hall of a noble lord and lady. Nine months later, each couple had a child, and those children grew up and had children, too. Some said that because of his time spent in the human world, all of humankind were descended from Heimdall—from the poorest servant to the most powerful ruler.

◊ Heimdall once fought with Loki in the shape of a seal and recovered Freyja's stolen necklace. Neither of these gods ever forgot their old feud, and Heimdall and Loki are destined to kill each other in the final battle between the giants and the Aesir.

◊ Heimdall owned a beautiful horse called Gulltoppr, which had a golden mane. He rode this shining steed to the assemblies and feasts of the gods, but he would leave the party early to return to his watch over the rainbow bridge.

TYR

GOD OF WAR AND BRAVERY, WHO LOST ONE HAND TO THE WOLF FENRIR

WHERE: *Wherever a battle is taking place or a brave deed is being performed*

Tyr was known as the "one-handed god," which was a compliment about his most famous act of bravery. In fact, Tyr was so admired for his courage that a day of the week—Tuesday—was named after him, as well as the runic letter "t." Tyr's mother was a giantess and some said his father was also a giant, like Loki's. However, unlike Loki, Tyr was always loyal to the gods.

Tyr lost his hand in the jaws of Fenrir the wolf, Loki's monstrous child. Odin thought that the best way to keep an eye on Fenrir when he was a wolf-cub was to keep him as a pet, and it worked out well . . . for a while. However, soon Fenrir grew so large that even Odin couldn't control him and Tyr was the only one brave enough to give him his dinner. But over time even brave Tyr became wary of the wolf's huge teeth and claws, and so the gods hatched a plan to tie him up. Odin had a special tether made by the dwarfs, which was as light and narrow as a ribbon, but stronger than anything in the world. The wolf suspected a trick was about to be played on him, and wouldn't agree to put on the leash unless a god would put their hand in his mouth. Tyr stepped forward without a moment's hesitation. The wolf agreed to have the tether put on him and was leashed and tied to a great rock. But when Fenrir realized he couldn't escape, he bit down hard on Tyr's hand and would not let go. The god lost his hand, but he didn't cry or complain one bit. That's how brave Tyr was.

◊ Tyr is fated to die fighting another ferocious creature, the hound Garm, which guards the entrance of Hel but will break free from his leash. Brave Tyr will not be scared in this fight either, even though he knows he will die.

◊ People who worshipped the Norse gods called the wrist the "wolf-joint" in Tyr's honor.

◊ Tyr's rune was sometimes carved on a sword in honor of this brave and battle-hardy god.

"Bold warriors used to pray to Tyr in the hope that he would help them out in battle, and that if they lost a limb they could be as brave as their hero."

"When fields of wheat were ready to harvest and blazed yellow under the summer sun, people were reminded of Sif and the beauty of her golden hair."

SIF

GODDESS OF WHEAT AND GOLDEN HAIR

WHERE: *In Asgard, at the heart of the family of gods*

Sif, the golden-haired goddess, was married to the red-bearded Thor. Sif's name means "marriage relation" and she helped to hold the family of gods together. She was most famous for her remarkable hair, and the light danced off her golden locks as she moved through the gardens and fields of Asgard. Anyone who saw her said her hair looked like bright gold, and they were right! Sif's hair was actually a wig of golden strands, but it wasn't always so . . .

As a young woman, Sif's hair was admired by all. It fell in long, blonde waves down her back, and when she walked it shimmered like a wheat-field in a gentle breeze. One day, Loki decided to play a trick on Sif and cut away her beautiful golden tresses while she was asleep. When Sif awoke and felt the tufts of hair where her beautiful locks had once been, she burst into tears. Once Thor got hold of Loki, the trickster god began to regret what they had done. "If you don't find a way to make things right, I'll break every bone in your body!" bellowed Thor. This time, Loki knew they needed to make up for their mischief and found the best metalworkers in the land of the dwarfs to make an extraordinary golden wig. It was so exquisite that Sif forgot all about her missing hair.

The most remarkable thing about Sif's wig was not how real it looked, but the fact that it grew just like natural hair! Sif carried an ever-growing fortune wound around her neck, and sometimes poets used "Sif's hair" to refer to gold itself.

◊ Sif was the mother of the archery god Ull, who was a child from a previous marriage. Thor made a good stepfather for this battle-keen boy.

◊ Some say that Loki was only able to get close enough to Sif to cut her hair because the two of them were secret lovers! However, this might just be a nasty rumor Loki started to get back at the gods.

◊ Thor's father Odin once teased his son at a river crossing, saying all kinds of horrible things to see how the red-bearded god would react. One of the things he said was that Sif had another lover in Asgard, and of all the insults this was most painful to Thor.

BRAGI & IDUN

GOD OF POETRY AND SONG, AND THE GODDESS OF YOUTH AND RENEWAL

WHERE: *In halls and at gatherings, and walking in the orchards of Asgard*

Bragi was the god with the charmed tongue. His voice was deep and clear, and he always found the right words whatever the occasion. He was the best poet in all the nine worlds, and there was no verse or song that he hadn't mastered.

Apart from his way with words, Bragi was known for his long beard, which reached almost to the floor. He was the husband of the ever-youthful Idun, and although his beard must have taken a lifetime to grow, he didn't look like an old man because of Idun's power to make those around her young.

Idun had smooth skin, glossy hair, and a bright smile: she was full of youth, and would remain that way forever. The source of her power lay in the apples of immortality that she gathered from a very special tree. She carried these apples with her at all times in a wooden casket, and as long as Idun shared these shining fruits with the other gods, they were also immune to old age. Even gray-bearded Odin had all the energy of a younger man, and he had been around since the beginning of the world!

The gods were reminded of Idun's power when she was stolen away by a giant eagle called Thiazi. Without Idun's apples, the gods found their joints growing stiff and their hair turning gray. Bragi hobbled around like the ancient being that he was. It was only when Loki swooped down into giant land in the form of a falcon and snatched her back that the gods regained their strength: the wrinkles fell from their skin, and their backs straightened.

◊ Poetry was very important to the Norse peoples and to the Vikings. A king was not worth anything if he didn't have a poet to sing about his victories and celebrate his journey to Valhalla when he died.

◊ Idun's name is very appropriate and means "forever young."

"Bragi must have composed hundreds of poems about his wife's beauty and the priceless gift she gave the gods."

NJÖRD & SKADI

AN UNLIKELY COUPLE

WHERE: *In the high mountains or by the shores of the ocean*

Njörd and Skadi were married, but they were not happy. In fact, you couldn't find a couple with less in common! For a start, Njörd was old—the oldest of the Vanir family of gods—and Skadi was young and a little wild. Njörd was the god of the ocean shore and its riches, and he was worshipped by sailors and fishermen. Skadi, on the other hand, lived in the high mountains far from the ocean, and she spent her days skiing and hunting with a bow. When Skadi skied, she moved as quickly as the shadow of a cloud passing through the mountains.

Skadi ended up marrying Njörd as compensation for the killing of her fierce giant father Thjazi. Odin allowed her to have her pick of the gods in marriage, but there was a catch: she would have to choose her husband just by looking at his feet! All the gods lined up behind a screen with just their feet poking out, and Skadi quickly chose the smoothest feet, thinking they must belong to the beautiful god Baldur. But she was wrong: the feet were actually old Njörd's! They were so smooth and clean because he was always walking barefoot through the waves.

At first, Skadi and Njörd tried to live together in her mountain realm, but after nine nights listening to thunderstorms and the howling wolves Njörd couldn't stand it any longer. They moved to Njörd's hall by the ocean, but Skadi couldn't sleep because of the crashing waves and crying seabirds. After nine more nights, Skadi returned home. They were better off living apart!

◊ Because the ocean is filled with fish and other creatures useful to humans, Njörd was known as a wealthy and generous god and his name was sometimes used to refer to someone who is very rich.

◊ Skadi's hall was called Thrymheim, the thunder home, because of the fierce storms that rolled through the mountains. Njörd's home was called Noatun, which means "ship enclosure": it was as close to the water as he could get!

"On clear days, Njörd could see up to Skadi's ice-capped mountains, and Skadi could see all the way down to the glistening ocean."

"Even the gods could not resist the temptation of bright gold, and it is the same in the world of humans to this day."

GULLVEIG

MYSTERIOUS GOLDEN WOMAN WHO ROSE UNSCATHED FROM FIRE

WHERE: *Moving between homes and teaching women magic arts*

Gullveig is the name of a stranger who came to Odin's hall during the happy days when the world was young. She was beautiful and shone like precious metal. The gold-hungry gods didn't hesitate in grabbing her, attacking her with their spears, and throwing her into a great fire—greedy to share out her golden remains. But even though the fire burned with an intense white heat, Gullveig stepped from it without a single mark on her. The gods were astounded. Three times they burned Gullveig, but every time she emerged as radiant as before.

When Gullveig rose from the fire for the third time, she took a new name, Heid, which means "bright." The gods knew that they had no choice but to let her go. She made her way to Midgard, the realm of humans, where she traveled from house to house practicing her magic in a trance, predicting the future, and teaching powerful spells to the women who lived there.

Some say that this golden woman was from the Vanir family of gods, who are extremely difficult to kill, and that her treatment by the Aesir gods may have been what provoked the war between the two families. However, the Aesir didn't know that when they threw her in the fire. It was pure greed that made them do such a horrible thing.

◊ The war between the Aesir and the Vanir might have been avoided if the Aesir had agreed to pay a fine for mistreating Gullveig. Instead they decided to go to war against a group of gods who were as hard to kill as the golden goddess, and that ended with neither side victorious and a truce between the families.

◊ Sorceresses such as Heid often carried a staff or wand. This was a sign of their power to see the future and perform magic arts.

◊ Gullveig means "gold-drink." She represented the intoxicating power of gold, which the greedy find very hard to resist.

THE CHILDREN OF THE GODS

THE MIGHTY CHILDREN OF ODIN AND THOR, WHO SURVIVE THE FINAL BATTLE

WHERE: *Shading their eyes from the sun in a wide green land*

Not all the gods are destined to die at Ragnarök. Some of the children of Thor and Odin will escape the destruction and go on to rule the new world that will rise from the ashes of the old.

Vidar, a son of Odin, was born with one purpose: to kill the wolf Fenrir and avenge his father's eventual death. In preparation Vidar wore a special boot with a reinforced sole. He is fated to step into the wolf's enormous jaws, so the boot had to be the strongest in the world!

Höd and Vali were also sons of Odin. When Höd, who was born blind, was tricked into killing his brother Baldur by Loki, the other gods ruled that he should be punished. So, Odin had another child whose task was to kill poor Höd: Vali was exceptionally powerful, and he killed Höd when he was only one day old! Vali is destined to survive Ragnarök, and Höd will return from Hel with Baldur. The brothers will walk arm in arm into the new world with no bad feelings.

Magni, Modi, and Thrud were children of Thor. Their names mean "the strong one," "the angry one," and "the powerful one." All three are fated to live on in the new world after Raganarök. Magni was only a toddler when he first showed how strong he was. He freed his proud father from under a giant's leg that was squashing Thor to death. Thor's daughter Thrud was as strong as her brothers and she was known for her amazing complexion, which was as pale as snow. Thrud was rebellious, and she once agreed to marry a dwarf named Alviss while Thor was away from home: Thor had to trick this dwarf into a battle of wits until the sun rose and turned poor Thrud's fiancé to stone!

◊ Not much is known about Modi, except that he and Magni will carry Thor's hammer between them into the new world. It will be a great protection if the monsters ever return.

THE STORY OF THOR'S HAMMER

The tale of Thor's hammer began when Loki cut off Sif's golden hair. Thor was so angry with Loki that he threatened to break every bone in the trickster's body if they didn't find a way to make things right!

Loki traveled to Svartalfheim and to the stone halls of the dwarfs who were the best at metalworking. The trickster paid two dwarfs to make a wonderful wig out of fine golden wires. Then, to make things right with the gods, Loki also asked the craftsmasters to make a gift for Odin and Freyr. Odin's gift was the spear Gungnir, and Freyr's gift was the ship Skidbladnir, which could be folded like a cloth and put in your pocket.

Loki was amazed at these gifts and became greedy. The god went to another workshop in the dwarf realm and spoke to a craftsman called Eitri and his brother Brokk. "If you can make three objects as magical as these," Loki said, showing them the wig, the spear, and the ship, "I'll let you take the head of great Loki as a prize." Brokk accepted the challenge and agreed to the price.

First, Eitri put a pig skin in the forge and told Brokk to keep the bellows going, no matter what. Even when a fly bit him hard on the hand, Brokk didn't flinch and Eitri forged a magnificent golden-haired boar, which could run on water and on land, and light the way at night.

Next, Eitri put gold in the forge. This time, even when the fly landed on his neck and bit him twice as hard, Brokk still kept the bellows going. Eitri presented Loki with a golden ring called Draupnir that would drip eight new golden rings every ninth night.

Finally, Eitri put iron in the forge and Brokk pumped the bellows. The fly, who was Loki in disguise, landed between Brokk's eyes and bit him hard. Wincing from the pain, Brokk stopped working the bellows for a moment to swat the fly away. Eitri presented Loki with Mjölnir, a magnificent hammer, but because Brokk had stopped working the bellows for just a second, the handle of the hammer was shorter than it should have been.

Loki and Brokk traveled back to Asgard and presented the treasures to the gods to decide which three items were best and who had won the bet.

All the gods agreed that while all the objects were valuable, the hammer Mjölnir was the most precious, even with its short handle. It would be the gods' secret weapon in their war against the giants.

Unfortunately for Loki, they had wagered their head and had lost the bet! But just before Brokk wielded his knife to chop off the god's head, Loki had an idea. "I promised you my head, but not my neck—you can have the one, but if you harm the other, you will break the deal and the gods will have you killed!"

No matter how hard he thought, Brokk could not come up with a way to cut off Loki's head without harming the god's neck, and he realized that he'd been outsmarted. Still, he could do what he liked to Loki's head, and before leaving the dwarf sewed the trouble-maker's mouth shut! The gods were relieved to have Loki silenced for a while, but all agreed that Loki had made amends for cutting off Sif's hair. A present goes a long way to make up for mischief, and when that present is the mighty hammer Mjölnir, almost anything can be forgiven!

THE STORY OF POETRY

The Norse gods loved to hear stories and songs when they were feasting in their halls, but they enjoyed poetry most of all, particularly if the poems were about themselves and their great deeds!

The story of poetry begins with the truce made between the Aesir and the Vanir gods, after a long and exhausting war between their families. They exchanged hostages and all spat into a bowl as a sign of their truce. Odin thought it would be a shame to let this spit go to waste, so he used spells to turn the liquid into a man. This spittle man's name was Kvasir. He was said to be the smartest being in all the nine worlds, but unfortunately he wasn't very good at judging whether someone was his friend or enemy, and it wasn't long before he was captured by two dwarfs. They drained all the liquid out of Kvasir and used it to brew three giant cauldrons of sweet mead: the famous honey wine drunk by the gods. This mead gave anyone who drank it the gift of poetry.

The dwarf brothers didn't get to enjoy the mead that they had made for long. They soon fell out with a giant named Suttung, who took the mead for himself. He hid it away in a cave beneath a huge mountain and ordered his daughter Gunnlod to guard it.

News of this reached Odin, and he headed in disguise to Suttung's mountain home to ask for a sip of the mead . . . but the giant laughed in his face. "Go home, graybeard," he said, "the mead is mine—every single drop!" Odin pretended to leave, but under the cover of darkness he used a drill to bore a hole right through the mountainside to the cave where Gunnlod was guarding the mead. He turned himself into a snake and slithered down into her room.

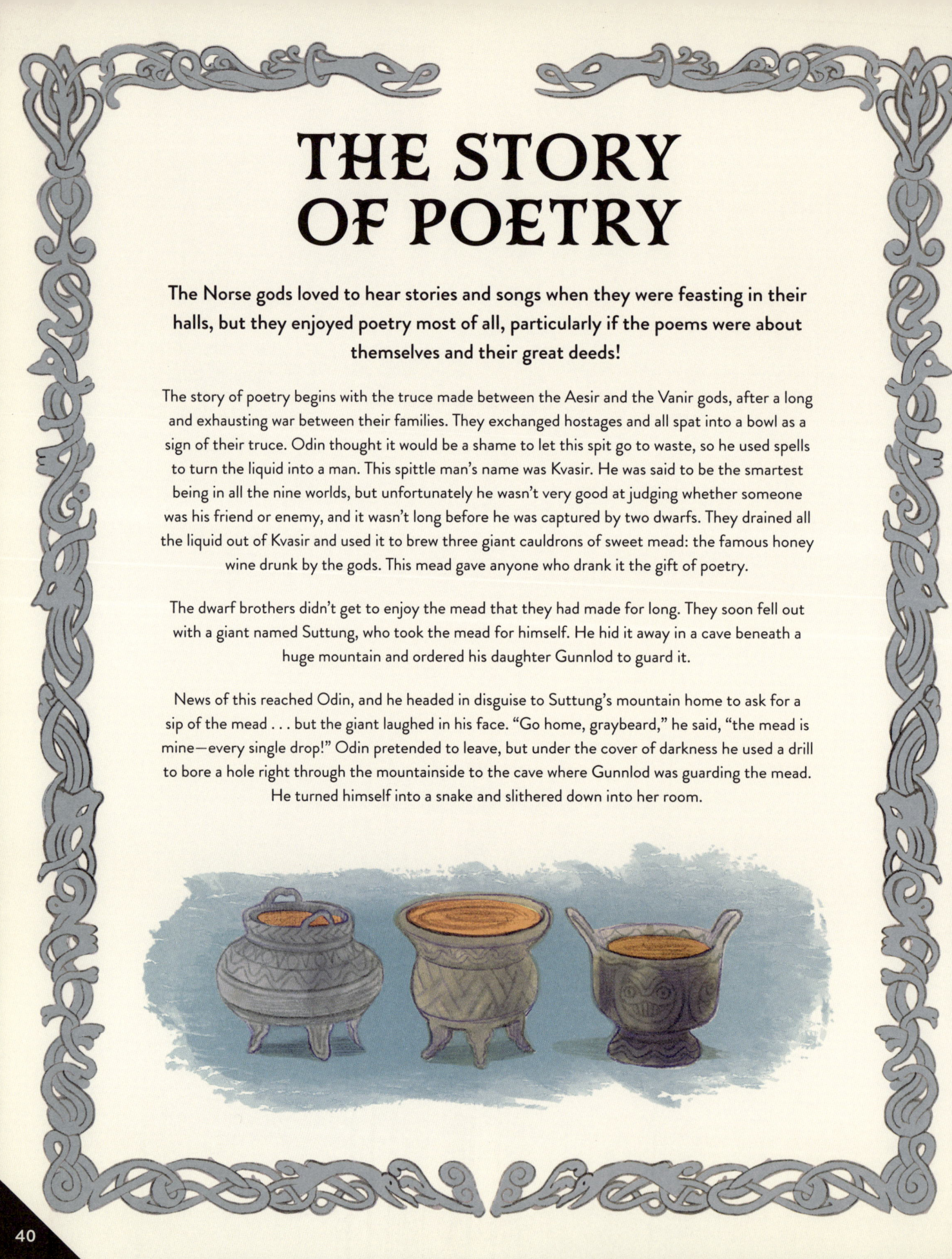

Gunnlod was so happy to have company that she agreed to everything Odin said to her. Each night Odin spent there, she let him have a sip of the mead, and Odin's sips were very big indeed—after three nights he'd drained all three cauldrons! As soon as he'd taken the last sip, Odin turned his back on poor Gunnlod and made his escape, turning into an eagle and flying away.

Suttung also turned himself into an eagle and chased Odin across giant land and into Asgard. As Odin swooped over the walls he spat out the mead into barrels that the gods had made ready. However, Suttung got so close to catching up with Odin on the way that the god accidentally blew a few drops of mead out of his bottom! It was said that these drops fell down to earth, and that anyone who writes bad poetry or sings bad songs is using this mead from Odin's backside! Better poets were given a share of the real mead of poetry, and when they were inspired they were said to be filled with the spittle, blood, and the amber mead of the gods.

GIANTS, MONSTERS, & MYTHICAL BEINGS

The great adversaries of the Norse gods were the giants, or jötnar. Giants were the first beings to emerge from the mists at the beginning of time, and the whole world had once been theirs to enjoy.

When the gods arrived and killed Ymir, they banished the surviving giants and their descendants to the edges of the world—to the high mountains, lava fields, and distant seas. Their realm was known as Jötunheim, and it was a desolate place of ice and jagged rocks, where storms blew out of nowhere: humans tried to avoid it at all costs.

The giants never forgot what the gods did to their ancestors, and they were always trying to get even. The power of the giants lay in the forces of nature that swept through the world: fire and gushing water, tumbling rocks, and freezing hail that battered crops. All that the gods built, the giants threatened to destroy.

When gods and giants met there was often fighting, but not always: giants had knowledge from the oldest times that the gods wanted to learn, and they owned powerful treasures. Giantesses gave birth to strong children, and they often married gods and became gods themselves: Thor's own mother was a giantess called Jörd, and she's probably the reason he was so sturdy and strong.

The giants may have been the enemies of the gods, but it was the monsters that Odin's family really feared. The three most terrifying monsters were all children of Loki: fierce Hel, who ruled the dead; Fenrir the wolf, who drooled a river from his jaws; and the Midgard-Serpent, who encircled the whole world. The gods were right to be afraid!

Some mythical beings were on better terms with the gods. The mysterious elves who lived in the brightest parts of the sky and the dwarfs who crafted precious things beneath the earth both helped Odin's family at times. The Norns who wove out the destiny of every living thing were neither friends nor enemies to the gods: they were beyond anyone's control.

AEGIR & RAN

GIANTS OF THE OCEAN AND ITS DESTRUCTIVE POWER; DEADLY TO SAILORS

WHERE: *In the deep ocean and in the waves that batter the shore*

Aegir and Ran were giants of the ocean, and—just like their watery home—they could be calm and generous to sailors, or fierce and deadly. Aegir was said to have a hall on the island of Hlesey in Denmark, but his wife Ran preferred open waters and the wild ocean.

Unlike most of the giants, Aegir had a good relationship with the gods. He once went on a journey from his island home to Asgard and he was welcomed as a guest. He ate good food, drank strong mead, and asked lots of questions about the world. Aegir felt he had been so well treated that he invited all the gods back to the island of Hlesey for a feast in his magnificent hall. The hall had no lighting, but Aegir took bright gold from his vast treasure hoard and spread it across the floor to light up the hall. Aegir was known for magic as well as riches, and at the feast the food and drink served itself! There was space for all the gods and elves, and everyone said that Aegir's hospitality was the best in the nine worlds.

Ran was very different to her husband. She owned a huge net that she used to trap sailors and drag them down to the bottom of the ocean. If someone was lost at sea, it was said that they had been taken into Ran's arms. The nine daughters of Aegir and Ran were all waves, and they had names such as "Rising," "Breaking," "Blood-haired," "Sky-bright," and "Roller." They could be good company to sailors, gently lapping against the ship's prow, or they could throw a boat around like a toy and thrash the shore in a tantrum. It was important to keep Ran and her nine fierce daughters on your side . . . or else the ocean was a very dangerous place to be.

◊ When Aegir came to Asgard, the gods put on a good show. They lit a hall with gleaming swords and decorated it with tapestries and brightly painted shields. They opened their finest mead and cooked the best food. No one could say that the Aesir were bad hosts!

◊ Aegir didn't have a cauldron big enough to brew beer for all the gods and elves, so the gods sent Thor to find one in giant land. He succeeded, but not without fighting a giant or two along the way!

At Aegir's feast, Loki brought the mood down by killing one of Aegir's servants. The poor lad had done nothing wrong: Loki was just upset that things were going so well!

"If old Njörd was a god of the shorelines and calm waters, Aegir and Ran held power over the wild open ocean, which even the gods couldn't control."

"Hrungnir was the giants' greatest champion: he was as tough as the hardest rocks of Jötunheim and as threatening as thunder in the mountains."

Hrungnir

A BRAWLING GIANT WITH A HEART OF STONE AND A WHETSTONE AS A WEAPON

WHERE: *On the rocky plains of Jötunheim*

Hrungnir was one of the most terrifying giants of all. His head and heart were made of the hardest stone, and he carried a polished rock as a shield and a huge whetstone as a weapon. On one fateful day, Hrungnir raced mighty Odin across the sky, each spurring their horses to gallop faster than the wind. When the riders reached Asgard, the gods followed the sacred laws of hospitality and offered the giant a drink. Hrungnir was not a pleasant guest and drank so much ale that he started to brag to the gods and then to insult them!

When Thor came home to find this badly behaved giant in the hall, he couldn't believe his eyes. He told Hrungnir that if he didn't leave that second, he would smash his stone head to smithereens! Hrungnir got unsteadily to his feet and staggered over to Thor. "If I had my shield and giant whetstone, I'd squash you flat!" he said. "I bet you wouldn't dare to face me if I was fully armed!" Even though his fingers itched to attack the giant then and there, Thor agreed through gritted teeth to single combat on the edge of giant land. The fight was on . . .

Beings came from across the nine worlds to watch the contest. The giants made a huge clay man to fight alongside Hrungnir, but Thor only took his quick-thinking servant Thjalfi. Thjalfi whispered in Hrungnir's ear that Thor was planning to burrow through the earth and come at him from below, and the giant believed him! Hrungnir placed his shield under his feet, sealing his fate. Of course, Thjalfi had lied! Instead of burrowing through the earth, Thor raced toward the giant, and swung his hammer just as Hrungnir threw his whetstone. The weapons collided with an almighty bang. The whetstone shattered into hundreds of pieces and one of these hit Thor in the temple knocking him to the ground in a daze. But the hammer struck Hrungnir right between the eyes and broke his great stone head in two.

◇ Thjalfi easily finished off the clay creature—it had been given the heart of a frightened horse and didn't stand much of a chance. The giants had nothing to brag about that day!

◇ Thor ended up stuck under one of Hrungnir's massive legs when the giant collapsed, and his son Magni was the only one strong enough to lift the leg off Thor. Magni was only three years old at the time! Thor gave him Hrungnir's horse as a thank you.

◇ The piece of whetstone that hit Thor stayed stuck in his temple for the rest of his life.

THRYM

A FEARSOME MOUNTAIN GIANT WHO STOLE THOR'S HAMMER

WHERE: *On his big estate in Jötunheim*

Thrym was a show-off who liked to have the best of everything. He stole Thor's hammer and hid deep underground: if Thor wanted to see his hammer again, the gods would have to give Freyja—the most beautiful woman in the world—as Thrym's bride.

No one could make Freyja do something she didn't want to, so Heimdall suggested that Thor dress up like the goddess, and pretend to marry Thrym. Thor didn't like this idea one bit, but what choice did he have? He scowled as Freyja squeezed him into a wedding dress, and put a veil over his face. Loki, never one to miss an opportunity for an entertaining afternoon, went along with Thor as his handmaiden.

Thrym was quivering with excitement when the guests arrived at the wedding. He sat the bride next to him, and the handmaiden Loki on the other side. Thor lifted his veil and scoffed all the food he could reach, followed by a whole roasted ox, and two barrels of mead! Thrym was a bit taken aback, but Loki reassured him that his bride had a big appetite. Later, Thrym lifted the veil to sneak a kiss . . . and saw Thor's eyes glaring back at him! "Don't worry," said Loki, "your bride hasn't slept since the engagement because she's so excited, that's why her eyes look so fierce."

After the feasting was over, Thrym ordered his servants to bring Thor's hammer out to bless the couple and seal the marriage. As soon as Thor caught sight of Mjölnir, he leapt up, and threw off the veil. Thor swung his hammer and bashed Thrym so hard that he tumbled right down to Hel. The god was so furious that he bashed all Thrym's wedding guests too—he wanted the giant to pay for stealing his hammer and making him sit there in a bridal dress. Neither Thor nor Thrym had a good time that day, but it was the best fun Loki had had in ages!

◊ Some people think this story was made up by Christians to mock Thor for wearing a dress, but the Norse peoples teased their gods as well as worshipping them, and they made them very like humans. Thor might have looked funny in a dress that was too small for him, but Loki was born to dress up and be whoever they wanted to be.

◊ Thrym was a bit of a poser. He had a herd of bulls with golden horns, and he kept a pack of giant dogs with golden collars with him at all times. He was used to getting his own way, but stealing Thor's hammer was a step too far!

◊ This wasn't the first or last time Loki took the shape of a woman. The god also turned themself into an old lady to find out Frigg's secrets. Frigg didn't notice that it was the same Loki she saw every day in Asgard!

UTGARDA-LOKI

A CUNNING GIANT WHO TRICKED THOR INTO A TRIAL OF STRENGTH

WHERE: *In his lava-field fortress*

Utgarda-Loki was a king among the giants. He lived in a huge stone fortress in the middle of a lava field. He was welcoming to guests, but he often challenged them to contests and used magic to win. Thor and his companions Loki and Thjalfi found this out to their cost when they visited the giant . . .

The first contest was between Loki and a servant called Logi. Loki chose an eating competition with the first to finish a trough full of food declared the winner. Loki ate as quickly as they could and the two opponents finished at the same time. But Logi had eaten up the trough as well as the food! It was 1–0 to the giants. Next, swift-footed Thjalfi chose a running competition. He ran three laps of a lava-field against an opponent called Hugi. Each time they raced, Utgarda-Loki's champion left Thjalfi farther and farther behind.

Thor chose a drinking competition and Utgarda-Loki gave him a long horn filled to the brim. "Too easy!" thought Thor. But he drank until his face was scarlet, and when he looked inside there was almost as much mead as before. Next, Utgarda-Loki challenged Thor to lift his giant cat off the floor, but no matter how high the god reached, the cat arched its back and kept three feet on the floor! Thor was angry and asked for a wrestling contest. The giant selected a frail old woman to wrestle with Thor, and no matter how hard he struggled, Thor could only get the woman to bend one knee.

The gods left Utgarda-Loki's fortress humiliated, but just as they were leaving the giant told them the truth. Loki had been in an eating contest with wild-fire. Thjalfi had been racing against the giant's own thoughts. Thor had wrestled with old age, which no one can defeat, and the cat he had been lifting was really the serpent that circled the whole world. He'd been drinking from a horn with one end in the ocean, and with his huge swigs, Thor had drained enough water to create the tides. The gods hadn't done badly at all!

◊ Útgard was the name of the lands outside the protection of Midgard, the world of humans. It was a desolate place of dark forests, broken lava fields, and soaring mountains, and it was where giants, trolls, and other fierce creatures lived.

◊ When the gods arrived at Utgarda-Loki's fortress, even mighty Thor wasn't able to push open the gate. But the gods were small enough to squeeze through the bars!

◊ When the gods left his fortress, Utgarda-Loki used sorcery to make it disappear into thin air. He'd seen the gods' power, and how Thor had almost beaten old age. He didn't want these guests coming back to find him!

GJALP & GREIP

POWERFUL GIANT SISTERS WHO TOOK ON THE MIGHTY THOR

WHERE: *On the border of Jötunheim and in their father's cavernous hall*

Gjalp and Greip were two fierce giantesses. They lived in their father Geirröd's rock-hewn hall, which was surrounded by cascading waterfalls. The sisters represented the power of the rivers in giant land—rivers that Thor had to cross to enter Jötunheim.

One time Thor was tricked by Loki into traveling to giant land without his hammer. The god came to a raging river that he needed to cross. Thor had a wooden staff and waded out using the staff to brace against the swirling waters. However, once he reached the middle of the river, the waters began to rise right up to Thor's neck. He looked up the valley and saw Gjalp standing on a rock and peeing into the river! A giant's pee is not a trickle but a powerful stream, and it mixed with the river to create a raging torrent. Thor had to think fast. He spluttered and coughed as he reached down to the riverbed and picked up a stone. Just as he was about to go under, he hurled the stone at Gjalp and knocked her into the river. With the waters stopped, he was able to scramble out by clutching at some overhanging rowan trees.

Unluckily for Thor, Gjalp's sister was just as fierce! When Thor reached the cavernous hall of Geirröd, he was led to a small cave outside the hall with a chair in the middle of the floor. Thor was glad to sit down after his fight with Gjalp, but no sooner had he sat than the chair started to rise toward the roof of the cave. Thor looked down and saw Gjalp and Greip under the chair. They were trying to crush him against the roof! The giantesses would have succeeded if Thor hadn't been carrying his wooden staff. He used it to push against the ceiling, and eventually pushed the chair back to the floor, with Gjalp and Greip pinned underneath it. Thor would never forget how close these giant sisters came to ending his life—and all in one short morning!

◊ When Thor finally made it into Geirröd's hall, he found that the father was no more welcoming than his daughters. The giant threw a red-hot bar of iron at Thor, who caught it in his iron gloves and threw it straight back. It pierced right through Geirröd, through the stone pillar behind him, and through the cave wall itself!

◊ The rowan tree was known to the Vikings as "Thor's protector." It is a small tree, but it has strong roots and is very hard to budge!

"Thor had so many battles with giants that he lost count: but few of them came closer to defeating him than the giant sisters Gjalp and Greip."

FENJA & MENJA

STRONG GIANTESSES WHO GRIND OUT THE SALT ON THE BOTTOM OF THE OCEAN

WHERE: *On the ocean floor, working their mill*

Fenja and Menja were two giantesses who were stronger than any human. They were captured when they were young and forced to work in the land of a human king, Frodi of Denmark.

In Frodi's kingdom there were two huge millstones that no one had been able to use for years because they were too large and heavy. Legend told that this mill would grind out whatever the king wanted, and Frodi ordered Fenja and Menja to test their strength. They pushed and heaved, and the stones began to turn. Instead of flour, pure gold fell from the mill. It made Frodi a very rich king indeed. He also asked the giantesses to grind out peace and wealth for his kingdom, and as long as the mill kept grinding, Denmark prospered.

Unfortunately, the more humans have, the more greedy they become. Frodi didn't let Fenja and Menja get any rest at all, and eventually, they got fed up. The giantesses started to grind out an army of fierce warriors from the mill. A sea-king called Mysing arrived to lead the millstone army, and they killed King Frodi and took all his treasure onto their ships.

King Mysing could have lived a long and prosperous life, but he was also greedy. He ordered the giantesses to grind out salt onto the deck of his longship. Fenja and Menja ground all day until there was a big pile of salt. But Mysing told them not to stop. So they ground and ground until the salt pile grew so heavy that it sank the ship. Fenja and Menja sank with the mill to the bottom of the ocean. With no one to tell them to stop, they are destined to keep grinding out salt forever.

◊ It was said that during King Frodi's reign someone could leave a gold ring lying on the grass, and nobody would even think to steal it because so much gold was ground out by the giantesses.

◊ The grinding of the mill created a giant whirlpool on the surface of the ocean, and if sailors saw it they would sail away from Fenja and Menja as fast as they could!

◊ The Norse peoples believed that it was Fenja and Menja grinding out salt from their mill at the bottom of the ocean that made the ocean salty.

"Giants were always powerful and dangerous to mess with, but in the case of Fenja and Menja, it was human greed that was most dangerous of all."

DWARFS

BEINGS OF THE ROCK AND WORKERS OF METAL AND STONE

WHERE: *Underground in their great stone halls*

The gods created the dwarfs very soon after the killing of Ymir and the creation of the world from his enormous body. They were an ancient people who inhabited the earth before humans, and they were very proud of their ancestry and knowledge of the past.

Dwarfs began life as sightless creatures burrowing around in Ymir's insides. Odin and his brothers decided that it was a waste for them not to have a purpose, so they gave them sight, speech, and intelligence. The dwarfs they created were wise and nimble-fingered, and enjoyed making precious things. They chose to live life underground and made their halls under rocks and mountains. Some dwarfs were so unused to the daylight that they turned to stone if they stayed out in the sun! Other dwarfs were happy living among humans and traveling between their underground realm of Svartalfheim and the lands above.

As metalworkers and smiths, the dwarfs had no equals. If humans found a splendid weapon or piece of jewelry, then they knew it must have been made by the dwarfs. Some of the gods' most precious objects were made by dwarf smiths. Odin's spear Gungnir, Freyr's ship Skidbladnir, and Sif's golden wig were made by the sons of a dwarf named Ivaldi, and they were all objects with great power. The golden boar, the ring known as "The Dripper," and Thor's mighty hammer were made by the dwarfs Eitri and his brother Brokk.

The dwarfs loved gold and guarded it jealously. When Loki stole the dwarf Andvari's gold hoard, Andvari cursed the treasure and made sure that anyone who owned it would meet a sticky end! Two dwarf brothers also killed the wise being Kvasir, just to take his knowledge for themselves. Even the gods had to tread carefully when they visited the dwarfs' stone halls.

◊ One Norse poem lists the names of important dwarfs. Some of these names—Gandalfr and Thorin; Bifur, Bafur, and Bömbur; Fili, Kili, and Oakenshield—have become famous because of English writer J. R. R. Tolkien's story *The Hobbit*.

◊ Four famous dwarfs were placed in the four corners of the world, and were given the job of holding up the sky. Their names are "North," "South," "East," and "West."

Dwarfs looked very much like humans. They could see well in the dark, and were strong and stocky from their stone-carving and blacksmithing.

"An object made by the dwarfs was very precious, but sometimes they asked for an unreasonable price . . . including Loki's head!"

"When all beings are remembered at the end of the world, Odin will be named the greatest of the gods, Yggdrasil the greatest of trees and Sleipnir the greatest of horses."

SLEIPNIR

ODIN'S EIGHT-LEGGED HORSE

WHERE: *Crossing between worlds, carrying the All-Father on his back*

Sleipnir was the finest horse found anywhere in the nine worlds. He had a beautiful gray coat and a shining mane, but there was something else that made him easy to recognize: his eight legs! Sleipnir had a very unusual beginning—Loki the trickster god gave birth to him! For once, Loki's antics didn't create a monster, but a wonderful creature that was admired by all the gods.

The story of Sleipnir's birth began with a giant builder who came to Asgard and offered to build a wall that would protect the gods from all intruders, including the giants. The builder wanted a high price for doing this work—both the sun and moon, and also the beautiful goddess Freyja. The gods agreed to this bargain, but reassured Freyja that the giant would never finish the work in the time they had given him: just one winter.

Unfortunately for the gods, the builder had a magic horse called Svadilfari. Svadilfari was able to drag huge boulders to the wall, and the giant then used his great strength to set them into place. The wall was being finished faster than any of the gods had thought possible and they began to panic. They decided to ask Loki for help and they soon had a plan.

The next day, Loki turned themself into a beautiful mare and galloped in front of Svadilfari. The Loki-mare neighed and shook her tail until the stallion broke free from his harness and ran after her into the woods. The builder couldn't finish the wall in time and to make matters worse, Thor came home, recognized the builder was a giant and sent him packing! A little while later, Loki gave birth to a special foal. It had eight legs and could outrun much larger horses. Odin named it Sleipnir and claimed it as his own. There would never be a better horse, or one with such unusual parents!

◇ Sleipnir was able to run across any terrain, and could even gallop across oceans and travel through the sky. He was also able to carry Odin down the long and treacherous road to Hel, and to return safely to the land of the living.

◇ It is lucky that the gods didn't have to give up the sun and moon or give Freyja to the giants. However, the builder didn't finish the wall either, and the gods' realm of Asgard was never completely protected against the giants. The bargain didn't work out well for anyone!

THE VALKYRIES

DIVINE WARRIOR WOMEN AND CHOOSERS OF THE SLAIN

WHERE: *Watching over every battle in the world*

The Valkyries were warlike women with the power to decide who died in battle. They wore gleaming chainmail and carried bright shields, and they rode down from the skies to the world of humans on swift horses. No matter how big or small the battle, the Valkyries would be there, like vultures circling a kill. They had already decided who they would carry off, and there was nothing the warriors could do to change their minds.

To be chosen to die in battle was not a bad thing. In fact, if the Valkyries chose a warrior to die, it meant that they had been picked to join the elite troops of the dead known as the Einherjar. These warriors lived their afterlife in Odin's hall Valhalla, or under Freyja's protection on the wide fields known as Folkgang. In Valhalla, the warriors would spend their days fighting with swords and spears. In the evenings, the chosen warriors feasted on long tables and were served cups of golden mead by the Valkyries. The mead came from the udders of a magical goat, and there was an endless supply. Odin always sat on the high table, overseeing the feast.

The Valkyries chose only the best warriors to join the Einherjar because they were preparing for battle with the giants at the end of the world. When Ragnarök comes and the monsters approach Asgard, the Einherjar will stand shoulder to shoulder with the gods and the Valkyries and face the darkness without fear. Ragnarök will be no place for cowards, so the Valkyries were very careful about the heroes they chose.

◊ Sometimes the Valkyries disagreed with Odin about which side should win a battle, or which warriors should die. One Valkyrie called Brynhildr disobeyed Odin and was forced to give up her powers and made to marry a human—the greatest punishment he could think of!

◊ The Valkyries had names that matched their ferocity, such as "Victory-driver," "Battle-noise," and "Spear-fight." Some of them had the power to turn into swans, and occasionally they appeared to humans as white-necked women in feathered robes.

"Elves liked to be given respect by humans, and could cause all kinds of illnesses and misfortunes if they were left out of people's prayers."

ELVES

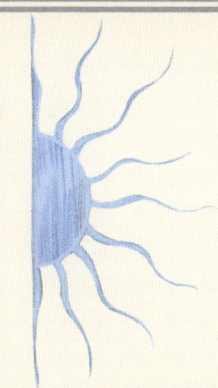

MYSTERIOUS BEINGS LIVING JUST OUT OF SIGHT

WHERE: *In bright Alfheim, or in the darkness of Svartalfaheim*

Elves were secretive and magical beings who were very close to the Aesir. They often joined the gods at their feasts, and humans prayed for the protection of the elves as well as calling on the help of gods.

The elves had two realms in the nine worlds. The light elves lived in shining Alfheim, high above the clouds. The god Freyr ruled over this bright land where the air was thin and the sunlight shimmered on the water. The elves who lived here were as dazzling as the light above the clouds. The dark elves lived in a very different place. Their realm was in the caves of Svartalfaheim, deep beneath the ground. Some said that they shared this underground realm with the dwarfs and that dark elves and dwarfs were hard to tell apart. They did not shimmer like their brothers and sisters in Alfheim, but their eyes shone like moonlight in the dark and they were very good at making precious things.

If someone was born with glowing skin and shining eyes, they were said to be "elf-bright." However, elves could also be sinister and do harm to humans. They were known to make horses nervous and farm animals weak. They also caused mental and physical illness in people. If someone had a stabbing pain, or if they were delirious with fever, it was said that they had been shot by elf-darts!

One famous elf was called Völund, and he was a prince among his people and the best craftsman in the nine worlds. One day, he was captured by a human king named Nidud and forced to make precious jewelry for the king and his followers. The king wounded the elf in the legs so he couldn't run away . . . but elves are dangerous beings to mess with. Völund killed Nidud's children and left the king a gruesome present: jewels made out of bones and body parts. He then flew to freedom on wings he'd made from swan feathers.

◊ Elves were in attendance at Aegir's feast, where Loki insulted everyone present and revealed all the gods' secrets. The gods were particularly embarrassed to have all their bad behavior spoken about in front of the elves!

◊ Many people were named after elves because of their nobility and power. The name Alfred means "Advised by the Elves," and the Scandinavian names Alva and Alf mean "elf."

◊ The realm of the light elves, Alfheim, was given to Freyr as a gift when he grew his first tooth. He is the god with the closest connection to these shining beings.

HUGINN & MUNINN

ODIN'S RAVENS "THOUGHT" AND "MEMORY"

WHERE: *Flying out across the nine worlds*

Huginn and Muninn were Odin's two beady-eyed ravens. They sat on the All-Father's shoulder or beside him on his throne in Valhalla, whispering their secrets into his ear. They were always ready to follow their master's orders and fly across the nine worlds in search of news.

Odin's ravens were not like other birds, though they looked the same and only Odin could really tell them apart. This made them very useful spies, since humans were not sure if the blue-black raven sitting in the tree or crowing from the top of a house was Huginn or Muninn, or just a regular bird. If the raven seemed to be watching as it circled above or peeped in at a door, it was best to be on guard.

Huginn and Munin's names mean "Thought" and "Memory," and wherever Odin's thoughts were, the ravens would be there too. He sent them out every morning at daybreak and they would return by breakfast time to tell him the news. They would bring tidings of wars brewing in the human world or tell him about love affairs. They noticed big things, but also the smallest details, which always gave Odin the edge when he visited the homes of kings or powerful giants. If an unexpected visitor in a gray cloak arrived at a hall, you could be sure that Huginn and Muninn had been there already, watching and listening, and learning all the household's secrets.

Although Huginn and Muninn were Odin's pets, all ravens had a connection with the god. They sensed when a battle was about to take place and they circled in the sky waiting for blood to be spilled. Huginn and Muninn were no different—they liked to peck at dead warriors and often they returned to Odin with their beaks glistening with blood!

◊ Odin also had two pet wolves, which he fed from his own plate at the high table in Valhalla. They were tame with Odin, but fierce with everybody else.

◊ The raven was sacred to the people who worshipped Odin. Vikings sometimes marched to war under a black and white raven banner. It fluttered in the wind and seemed to bring the raven to life.

◊ The connection between Odin and Huginn and Muninn was so strong that he was often called the god of ravens. Gold amulets worn by his followers showed a god on horseback carrying a spear and with two ravens flying overhead.

THE NORNS

WOMEN OF FATE WHO WOVE OUT THE FUTURE OF EVERY PERSON

WHERE: *Beneath the roots of the World-Tree by the Well of Fate*

The women known as the Norns controlled the destiny of every living being in the world. They decided who would live a good life and who would suffer from misfortune. Even the gods were powerless to change the future that had been set by these three mysterious women.

The names of the Norns were Urd, Verdandi, and Skuld, and they knew everything that had happened in the past, everything that was happening in the present, and every single thing that would happen in the future. They lived in a beautiful hall beneath the roots of Yggdrasil, the mighty tree that grew through the nine worlds. Next to their hall was a deep well fed by a spring and overhung with dripping roots. Here, the three women had set up a loom for weaving. But instead of weaving cloth or tapestries, the Norns wove lives together and spun out the destinies of heroines and villains, farmers and kings. Once the Norns wove out a person's fate, it could not be changed and once they cut the thread, it meant that death was certain.

There was one other task that fell to the Norns. As well as weaving out the fates of gods and humans, they were responsible for looking after the World-Tree itself. Every day Urd, Verdandi, and Skuld would take water from the spring, mix it with clay and mud, and rub it on the roots and trunk of the mighty tree. This helped to protect Yggdrasill from damage and decay. Without the careful attention of the Norns, the tree would rot, and the whole universe would topple and fall back into the abyss.

◊ Sometimes people who had bad luck would curse the Norns and feel that they had been badly treated. But the Norns were not interested in people's feelings or curses. They simply wove, without hatred or love for the people whose lives they were touching.

◊ Some said that there were Norns for each type of being in the nine worlds—Norns for the elves, Norns for the dwarfs, Norns for the giants, gods, and humans. No being could escape from fate, no matter how powerful.

◊ Norns were often said to be present when a child was born. From the moment that they drew their first breath, Urd, Verdandi, and Skuld had chosen the infant's destiny and whether they were to live a heroic life and die young in battle, or live to a ripe old age.

"Odin might get his pick of the warriors who died in battle, but Hel took most of the dead, and for this reason some say she was more powerful than any god."

HEL

CORPSE-FACED RULER OF THE UNDERWORLD

WHERE: *Ruling the underground realm of the dead*

Hel was the monstrous daughter of Loki. Odin sent Hel down to rule over the miserable realm of the dead far beneath the roots of the World-Tree. The land of the dead took her name and it is also called Hel.

It was easy to recognize Hel. Half of her body was blue-black like a bruise and the other half was as pale as a corpse. She walked with hunched shoulders and was always very gloomy. Hel guarded the dead very closely, helped by her huge dog Garm. The road to Hel's realm led down through treacherous caverns and over a raging river crossed by a slender bridge. There was only one entrance and the gates opened only one way: from the land of the living and into the land of the dead.

Everyone who died from old age or sickness would end up in Hel. The only way to escape this fate was to die in battle and be taken by the Valkyries to sit beside the gods in Valhalla. Hel's own hall was called "Drizzle Damp," and at its entrance there was a step called "Stumbling." No matter how many people filled the hall there was always space for many, many more.

There was nothing pleasant about Hel, but within the realm of the dead there was one place that was especially bad. This was where murderers and oath-breakers would go. They would have to cross streams full of knives to a grim hall called "Corpse-Shore," which was dark and damp and woven from serpent spines. The roof leaked and so much poison dripped down from the rafters that a foul river flowed from the hall.

◊ Hel owned a special bowl called "Hunger" and a knife called "Famine." Her sleeping place was known as "Sick Bed" and the drapes that surround it were called "Glistening Illness." Her two servants were called "Lazy" and "Foot-dragger," and they were no better than their names suggest.

◊ The most famous residents of Hel's hall were the shining god Baldur, killed by his brother, and Baldur's wife Nanna, who died from grief. They were served well, as they waited to rejoin the young gods after Ragnarök.

◊ The population of Hel's realm was always growing, and it will keep growing until Ragnarök comes and the dead are unleashed on the land of the living.

JÖRMUNGAND

THE SERPENT THAT ENCIRCLED THE WORLD IN ITS COILS

WHERE: *In the depths of the ocean that surrounds Midgard*

Down in the murk of the encircling ocean waters lay Jörmungand, the Midgard-Serpent. He fed on all the dead things that fell to the bottom of the ocean and he grew so large that eventually he encircled the whole world in his coils and bit down on his own tail.

Jörmungand was not always so large and ferocious. Like Hel and the wolf Fenrir, the Midgard-Serpent was the child of Loki. Whereas Odin tried to raise the wolf himself and banished Hel to the underworld, he threw the small serpent out into the deep ocean where he thought that the monster could do least harm. But that was a big mistake. In the endless space of the ocean, Jörmungand grew and grew until he was so large that there was nothing bigger in the world.

Jörmungand's great adversary was the mighty Thor. Thor won all his battles with the giants, some of whom were the size of mountains. However, the Midgard-Serpent was a different enemy entirely. The prophesies said that Thor will face Jörmungand at Ragnarök and that Thor will kill the serpent. But there is a catch: Thor will also die from the serpent's poisonous breath. The red-bearded god will finally meet his match.

Thor met the serpent once before the fatal battle at the end of the world. He went fishing for him using an ox-head as bait and used all his divine strength to drag the serpent to the surface. Thor would have smashed his hammer on the serpent's head, if his companion Hymir hadn't cut the fishing line. Some said that if Thor had not been stopped he would have killed the monster there and then. However, others said that the serpent would have thrashed about so much before it died that it would have flooded the whole world.

◊ The Norse peoples believed that a deep ocean surrounded the whole world, and that Jörmungand had wound his way along the ocean floor to create a complete circle. For this reason, he was known as the "Belt" of the World.

◊ It was prophesized that at Ragnarök the Midgard-Serpent will let go of its tail and unravel itself. As Jörmungand slithers onto the land, the oceans will break from their place and cause great tidal waves to flood the land.

"Somewhere in the depths beneath Thor's little rowing boat lay Jörmungand, disturbed from his long sleep and rising darkly to the surface of the ocean."

"Fenrir was the most ferocious wolf the world would ever know: his jaws were large enough to blot out the light from the sky, and the drool from his mouth gushed like a swollen river."

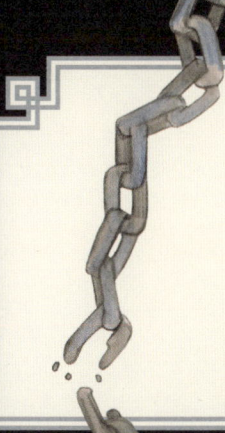

FENRIR

THE INFAMOUS WOLF THAT WILL END ODIN'S LIFE

WHERE: *On an island in a rust-colored lake, straining at his leash*

Fenrir was known across the world as the terrible wolf and the monstrous son of Loki. He was raised as a cub by Odin, even though the All-Father knew that the same wolf was destined to kill him in the final battle.

Odin kept other wolves as pets and when he visited the human realm, even the most aggressive dog would slink away with its tail between its legs. However, Fenrir was no normal wolf and grew so large that even Odin couldn't control him. All the gods except brave Tyr were afraid of Fenrir and there was no sign that he would stop growing.

Odin decided that Fenrir needed to be leashed, so he asked the dwarfs to make a heavy chain. Fenrir allowed the gods to wrap the chain around him to test his strength, but with a heave of his muscles, Fenrir shattered it. Next, Odin asked for an even heavier chain. It took several of the strongest gods to carry it to Fenrir, but once again, the wolf arched his back and broke free. Now, Odin knew that magic was the only thing that would restrain the wolf. He asked dwarf craftsmen to make a leash from six of the hardest things to find: the sound of a cat's footsteps, the roots of a mountain, the breath of a fish, the spit of a bird, the sinews of a ferocious bear, and the beard of a child! The leash was called Gleipnir and it was as light as a ribbon.

Fenrir suspected a trick when the gods led him to an island in a lake to test his strength against Gleipnir, so he made Tyr put his hand in his mouth while the gods tied him up. As hard as Fenrir strained, the thin leash would not break and the wolf bit down on Tyr's hand when he knew he'd been deceived. The gods used two huge stones to anchor the leash in place, and when Fenrir lunged at them with his jaws open, the gods stuck a sword upright in his mouth. It was said that Fenrir drooled so much from his open jaws that it caused a river to flow from the lake!

◇ The chains used to tie Fenrir up were called Laeding and Dromi. There was a saying "to break out from Laeding" or "to break free from Dromi," which meant to complete a difficult task!

◇ When Fenrir breaks free at Ragnarök, he will bring carnage to the world. His mouth will gape so wide that his lower jaw will drag on the ground and his upper jaw will block out the light from the stars. Nothing in his path will be spared.

◇ Odin always knew that Fenrir would kill him in the final battle. But he also knew that his silent son Vidar would avenge his death, stepping into the wolf's jaws with his specially made shoe to deliver the killing blow.

"When Surt leaves his post and marches on the world, it will look like a blazing sun advancing across the encircling ocean."

SURT

A GIANT FROM THE LAND OF FIRE WHO WILL BURN THE WORLD WITH HIS FLAMING SWORD

WHERE: *Guarding the borders of the fiery realm of Muspellsheim*

Muspellsheim was the fiery realm that melted the ice of Ginnungagap at the beginning of the world. It lay far to the south and it was not a place that gods or humans could go. In fact, it would have scorched anyone who wasn't born in the furnace-heat of Muspellsheim: even frost giants and trolls would have been burned to a crisp!

Surt was the name of the fire giant who guarded the borders of Muspellsheim. He carried a flaming sword that blazed like the light of a terrible sun. Surt was as large as any giant, charred all over his thick skin, and with eyes that were like glowing embers taken straight from a fire. When a volcano erupted and lava poured from a crack in the earth, it was like seeing Surt advancing from beneath the earth with his blazing sword.

When Ragnarök comes, and the giants battle with the gods, it will be the giants of Muspellsheim who will bring most destruction to the world. Surt will lead a great host up from the land of fire to the realm of the gods, and his sword will burn so brightly that it will set everything in his path ablaze. Even the rainbow bridge will collapse after Surt crosses into the realm of the gods.

Surt is destined to fight with Freyr in the final battle. Freyr will be missing his famous sword which fought by itself, and he will have to fight this terrible enemy armed only with the antler of a stag. Freyr will put up a good fight, but he will be no match for Surt who will surround him in flames. With Freyr fallen, Surt will have nothing to stop him, and he is fated to set the whole world on fire.

◊ Surt means "the charred one," which is an appropriate name for a giant who guards the land of fire and carries a flaming sword.

◊ When Surt burns the world with his fire, everything is destined to be destroyed. But from the ashes of his fire, a new green world will emerge: just like the moss and grass that grow on black lava fields.

◊ There is a volcanic island near Iceland named Surtsey, or Surt's island. It erupted from the seabed and created a great plume of ash and steam that could be seen for miles around.

THE STORY OF RAGNARÖK

This is the story of how the gods believed their world would end, in a battle with giants and monsters that would burn the sky and plunge the nine realms into darkness. Some say that Ragnarök has already happened, but others believe the gods are still with us: waiting for the end of the world and their inevitable defeat.

The first sign of Ragnarök will be three terrible winters in a row with no summers to melt the snow. There will be great wars between the peoples of the world and families and friends will turn on each other. It will be an age of knives and wolves and fierce howling winds. Then three red cockerels will crow all at once, and the gods will know without a doubt that worse is on its way.

The wolves chasing the chariots of the sun and moon will finally catch up with their prey. They will swallow the sun and moon whole and plunge the world into darkness. The earth will shake, trees will be uprooted, mountains will crumble, and the chains of all prisoners will break. The wolf Fenrir will run free with his huge jaws gaping wide, and the Midgard-Serpent, Jörmungand, will let go of his tail and emerge from the ocean with great waves crashing around him.

From fiery Muspellsheim, Surt will lead the giants to Asgard. He will approach the rainbow bridge brandishing his flaming sword and Heimdall will blow his horn to warn the gods that the final battle is about to begin. Loki will also break free and will lead an army of the dead so large that it cannot be counted.

Odin and his hand-picked warriors will emerge from Valhalla and prepare themselves for battle. Winning is out of the question, but these heroes will face the forces of chaos without fear. Odin will be swallowed by Fenrir, but his son Vidar will step into the wolf's jaws and avenge his father with a mighty sword thrust. Thor will battle the Midgard-Serpent, killing it with a blow from his hammer, but taking just nine steps backward before dropping dead from its poison. Loki and Heimdall will fight hand to hand and they will kill each other with fierce sword blows.

Surt will take on Freyr and the god of fertility will die surrounded in flames from the fire-giant's sword. Surt will set fire to the rainbow bridge, the wolves will howl in their victory, and the old world will sink as black smoke blots out the stars.

But all will not be lost, even as the world burns. The youngest of the gods will find a safe place to hide, and when the smoke clears they will walk back to the plains of Idavoll and find a golden hall in a land that is already turning lush and green under a bright new sun. Modi and Magni will carry Thor's hammer to Idavoll and be greeted by Baldur and his wife Nanna, returned from the dead. The god Höd will also be there, with the shy god Hœnir and the children of Odin. They will tell stories of the old world as they play in the green meadows.

Two humans will also survive by climbing in the branches of the World-Tree, which will be scorched, but alive inside its burned bark. The rivers of this new world will be full of fish and crops will grow without being planted. It will seem like the perfect start for a new world . . . but on the horizon there will be a shadow: the dragon Nidhög flying up from the dark hills of his underground lair. There will always be monsters for the gods to battle, even in this bright new land.

GLOSSARY

adversary – an enemy or opponent

Aesir – the main family of gods

Alfheim – one of the nine realms, the home of the light elves

Asgard – one of the nine realms, the home of the Aesir

bellows – a tool used to blow air into a fire

Bifrost – the rainbow bridge connecting the worlds of humans and gods

charred – burned or scorched

divine – godlike

hall – a large wooden building where people live, sleep, and feast

handmaiden – a female helper or servant

Hel – one of the nine realms, the home of the dead, and the name of its ruler

hostage – a person taken captive to ensure the other side sticks to their promises

Idavoll – the outdoor meeting place of the gods

Jötunheim – one of the nine realms, the home of the giants

Midgard – one of the nine realms, the world of humans

Muspellsheim – one of the nine realms, the realm of fire

Niflheim – one of the nine realms, the realm of ice and mists

oath – a solemn promise

rune(s) – the ancient letters used by the peoples of Northern Europe

sinew – a tendon (a strong part of the body that connects muscle to bone)

staff – a strong wooden stick

Svartalfheim – one of the nine realms, the home of the dwarfs

tether – something used to tie up an animal

truce – an agreement to stop fighting

Utgard – the outer lands, beyond the protection of the gods

Valhalla – Odin's golden hall where the chosen warriors feast

Valkyries – divine warrior women who collect the bodies of dead warriors

Vanaheim – one of the nine realms, the home of the Vanir family of gods

Vanir – the smaller family of gods led by Njörd

whetstone – a stone used for sharpening tools such as knives